Women Supporting Women:
Redefining Friendship, Tribe, and Community

Nancy Whitman Klotz

Copyright © 2020 Nancy Whitman Klotz

All rights reserved. This book or any portion
thereof may not be reproduced or used in any
manner whatsoever without the express written
permission of the publisher except for the use of
brief quotations in a book review.

ISBN: 9798624658240

To my family, friends, students, and community of women.

Contents

Introduction: Community Changes Our Lives	3
Chapter 1: Why Women?	12
Chapter 2: Finding Your Community	19
Chapter 3: The Community for You	25
Chapter 4: What Communities Have in Common	33
Chapter 5: How Communities Grow and Evolve	44
Chapter 6: How to Know if You've Outgrown Your Community	54
Chapter 7: When the Community Isn't a Good Fit	60
Chapter 8: Starting a New Community	63
Chapter 9: Joining a Community	66
Chapter 10: The Life of a Community	76
Chapter 11: Transient Communities	80
Chapter 12: Community as an Entity	86
Chapter 13: Is Joining a Community Worth It?	91
Chapter 14: Your Community Go-forward Plan	93
Conclusion: Community Makes Your Life Full	96
About the Author	101

Acknowledgements

Thank you, God.

Thank you to all the women with the stories they shared for this book.

Thank you to my classes and students who contributed to the idea that community is a topic that needs to be promoted and acknowledged.

Thank you to my community of like-minded women who want to improve their well-being through acts of self-care.

Introduction:
Community Changes Our Lives

Would you like to make a difference in someone's life? Are there times when you wish someone would step in and make a difference in your life? Would you provide direction and inspiration for each other?

This book shares stories about women connecting and finding each other, helping us to transform and deepen our approach to life. I have found that I need women in community in order to let go of the past and navigate the future. I feel stronger knowing a group of women has my back and will stand with me through happy times, struggles, and challenges. This book is not meant to influence you or to talk you into a way of life. My intention is to share experiences and provide opportunities for growth, support, and collaboration with other women, knowing that you matter. You matter.

We, as women, are social beings who want to be heard. By creating strong bonds with each other, women have a positive effect on our own health and wellness. We get stronger by getting to know each other, and by sharing who and what we are. As women gather, we form our own kind of energy including offering camaraderie and support, lifting each other up, and providing opportunities for growth. We have the ability to connect by sharing stories, celebrations, and struggles. Combining our strengths and collaborating with one another allows us to be inspired, choose our own way, and find our voices. We can tell each other the truth even if it is uncomfortable and pick each other up when we've gone off course.

The power of women connecting and supporting each other helps you feel less alone and better equipped to face life's challenges. You get to know each other and share experiences. Closeness and interaction help pave the way for us to move forward in life in a positive direction.

Did you ever have something wonderfully exciting happen in your life, but you weren't sure who to celebrate it with? Would you celebrate a new job with a neighbor who has been out of work for two years? Would you celebrate a big purchase with a miserly old relative? Who would get the excitement you want to share?

Your kind of person – one with similar interests – would understand your excitement. Your wins in life can be comfortably celebrated with a group of like-minded people. Sharing your wins with a community who understands you is uplifting and positive.

If you weren't sure of how to solve a problem, would you be open to having a group of like-minded women help direct you? You may have picked up this book because you have a problem in your life that you are not certain how to solve. You may not be able to identify the problem clearly or know of a solution to try. Who would you problem-solve with? Would solving it alone, with a friend or tribe, or with a community work best for you?

Here are my descriptions of being **alone**, being part of a **tribe**, and being part of a **community**.

You could muscle your way through to the end of the problem **alone**. This may include research, trial and error, and overcoming your uncertainty and fear of the unknown. Do you feel like you have no one to turn to? You may think you need to go it alone. Do you feel like you need to do everything yourself, even if someone else offers to help? You may think you know yourself best and would figure the way through the problem in your own best interest. On the other hand, do you feel compelled to turn to someone in your life even though you think they aren't the right person for the job? Someone else might expect that you share your worries with them, even if they aren't qualified to help you.

What about a **friend**? Do you have a friend who will understand your problem or help you find possible solutions? A friend is someone you have a close relationship with, someone you know personal information about who also knows many of your private thoughts and opinions. A friend is someone that you trust and believe. You bond with this person and treat them as a companion. You may share life stories with a friend and try to work through situations comfortably and without judgment. Would your friend be the most prepared person to get you through your challenge?

What are your thoughts about a **tribe**? Your tribe is a group of your friends or contacts. You may have different tribes for different parts of your life, such as work, family, or hobbies. Even though you know each person individually, they may not know each other well. The people in your tribes may not have synergy as a group or with each other. In this case, you would connect with one or two people at a time, talk about your problem, and listen to their opinions. Are people in your tribe the most qualified or knowledgeable people regarding your specific issue?

There is another choice: **community**. This is a group of like-minded women coming together to support each other for a specific purpose. Community is not only physical, but emotional and psychological as well. It can be viewed as a group of women gathering and communicating for a common reason or objective. A sense of community develops when you know that your group has your back and will provide the support you need as you move through your situation. Community gives you a sense of belonging and the confidence to move through uncertain times. Interestingly, you can ask a question of community and get several answers back from different people who are familiar with your topic or life experience.

You may start out in community and create relationships or friends from individuals in the community. How would you develop trust in the community? Trust takes time, observation, and interaction. The life of the community needs to feel right in your gut, your intuition.

Community also provides the opportunity to take on different roles: being a **mentee**, who gets advice from someone with more experience; and being a **mentor** to someone with less experience, as you share possibilities with them.

> "Women empowering other women.
> They get the psycho-social support. They become part of a community."
> — Annie Lennox

Community is important to me because I don't want to feel alone moving through life. I want to live life with more confidence and ease, knowing that I have the support I need to take the next right step. If the step fails, I will have a group to pick me up and encourage me to move forward again. With community, I like to use the words belonging, confidence, positive, learning, sharing, energy, authentic, connection, and trust. I want to share the power of community with you.

Let's take an example.

Donna has **friends** from elementary school and college whom she keeps in occasional contact with. Even though Donna is single, some of her friends are married, have children, and don't work. She has a **tribe**, which includes people she works out with at the gym. Some members of the tribe work from home and others work for bigger corporations. She also belongs to a business mastermind that organizes members into business groups, including one for entrepreneurs and startups.

Donna is an entrepreneur starting a company that develops mobile apps for other businesses that want to expand their services to their customers. For all of her business scenarios and questions, Donna has a **community** to count on to share their experiences with her. From this group, she gets her professional needs met. She can celebrate business goals that she reaches, and establish new, realistic business goals. She may make some friends in the group whom she spends time with outside of the community.

When Donna has an issue regarding relationships or health – things outside the scope of this community – she has friends and tribes to talk to. She could also find another community to help her meet those specific needs. This example may seem simplistic, but Donna's needs are being met!

What needs do you currently have? Can you identify any communities that you currently belong to? If you reflect, where do you fall with respect to connectedness to other women? If you put yourself on a continuum, do you have a community, a tribe, or a friend? Or are you alone?

I am writing to you – the woman, the friend, the part of my tribe and community who feels stress and anxiety from life and its experiences. I am reaching out to you so we can explore what having a community of women brings to our lives. How does community help shape our authentic selves (ourselves without all the barriers up)? Whether we are students, single women, new moms, divorced women, empty nesters, or aging-parent caregivers, we all have a common thread running through our lives. We are familiar with the past and need to navigate the future. How can community help us transition through phases in life? Growth can be unsettling and taking the first step forward can cause doubt and fear. Taking the first step is also courageous. Depending on where you are in life and what you are transitioning to, community can provide experiences that support both the current and next phase in your life.

How do we benefit from communities that support us? We are more confident moving forward in a positive direction when we feel supported. We get ideas and direction from our group. How are we supportive to other women in our own community? We share our experiences and stories to help lift them up, being a catalyst for change. I heard an analogy once of a person reaching down with one hand to pull someone up, while holding up the other hand to be pulled up by someone else. This is what it means to be in community.

> "The way to achieve your own success is to be willing to help somebody else get it first."
> — Iyanla Vanzant

Have you ever felt a void in your life that needed filling, even if you couldn't define that void? It may be a feeling of emptiness or "not knowing." Community is like having a best friend whom you don't see for years and picking up the relationship where you left off. The relationship feels casual and easy. Community is knowing that someone has your back when you need the support, helping you feel stronger and more confident. It is an unspoken feeling that consistently surrounds your soul with a sense of security and confidence. You can't reach out and touch community, but it's always in the background, waiting to understand you and your life.

Community is a joint force of energy reaching out to push life in a positive direction. It is a combination of effort to live life with more ease. Your ability to connect and collaborate feels like everything will be all right in the end. You have an accepting relationship with each other, learning to accept yourself and letting go of judgment.

Women Supporting Women:
Redefining Friendship, Tribe, and Community

Community is a life force that has a way of repairing, protecting, and developing itself. When you are ready, you will see a solution, even if it is just the smallest of steps. You will be lifted up, not let down. Community meets you where you are, knows where you want to be, and helps to get you from here to there. It is all-encompassing, allowing you the luxury of being yourself.

Allow the idea of community to settle in with yourself and pay attention to how you feel with a sense of community in your life. Being part of a community that is right for you is a great backup if you feel uncertain, have questions, or want to share a celebration! How do you know if the community is right for you? Pay attention to the support you feel, and the confidence you have in the group's advice, ideas, and actions. You have the opportunity to give and receive knowing that you don't have to walk through life alone.

What are ways you can use community? You can learn, solve problems, share celebrations, network, find support, meet new friends, enjoy spending time with one another, mentor other people, get mentorship, have fun, find a sense of belonging, know you're not alone, share similar experiences, and unload anxiety and uncertainty. That's the power of community!

Chapter I:
Why Women?

Culturally, women have been expected to care for and nurture others more than themselves. We put others first. Studies have shown that social bonding is an integral part of human nature and is a part of our brain from an evolutionary standpoint. Social support is typically based on shared values or interests between members, and a sense of belonging is essential to our development as healthy participants in society.

Studies also show that women communicate more easily than men do, both verbally and non-verbally[i]. They connect with each other by being totally themselves and digging deep emotionally. They bond informally and instinctively without judging. They encourage and support each other. "Always being there," "being oneself," and "trust and loyalty" are emphasized as important parts of women bonding.

Isolation has become more common as technology, social media, and texting has advanced, leaving out the personal interaction that is necessary in relationships. Loneliness has been identified as a factor in a variety of health issues. By maintaining social connections, women actually increase oxytocin – a hormone that helps with calming, reducing stress, and bonding. Women help each other's wellness by nourishing each other and maintaining friendships with uncomplicated acceptance.

Does that mean that no women put their own self-interest first? Or that some women wouldn't think twice about pulling someone down to build themselves up? No. For example, there was a time when the competitiveness of women entering the workforce brought other women down. Another example is when women compare themselves to determine who is higher or lower on the scale. Not comparing is the way to be our authentic selves. But as a whole, we need to support each other to move forward with confidence and ease. Now, women are realizing that we are stronger when we connect and collaborate.

> "A woman is full circle. Within her is the power to create, nurture, and transform."
> – Diane Mariechild

I have heard women in community referred to as sisterhood, girl squad, and the new family. By finding a group of women with similar interests and values, you can hang together and help each other share, trust, and move forward in a positive direction.

A community is a group of like-minded individual women sharing similar experiences. There is an ebb and flow in the dynamics of the group as one person has struggles and another feels content. You can imagine a community as a moving, feeling entity that changes as your needs in life change. The members are interdependent pieces of the community. At some point, you are the person with the hard challenges; another time, you are able to support someone else through their difficult times.

You may find more benefit from the group at a particular crossroads in your life, such as being single or getting married. You may benefit from helping another woman who is at a phase in life that you have already passed through, like getting divorced or having a baby. Your community may take on a life of its own as the members sync and bond with each other. Use someone else's strengths to fill your weaknesses, as you, in turn, support another woman.

> "Friendship of a kind that cannot easily be reversed tomorrow must have its roots in common interests and shared beliefs."
> – Barbara Tuchman

Common Roadblocks

Whatever our differences, women feel similar emotions. We often get stuck in common roadblocks when change is necessary. We can't always be prepared or plan for life changes. Sometimes we don't know the questions to ask. Our heads and our hearts are not in the same place. We may be living in a way that is against our value system. We might feel self-criticism, resistance to change, overwhelmed, or stuck. We might feel a need for purpose.

Self-criticism is our constant companion. It is self-defeating and keeps us from moving forward. Self-criticism is about blaming ourselves or getting caught up in our mistakes until we degrade ourselves. We tend to give negative experiences more value than they deserve. Thoughts go around and around, ruminating in our minds. Have you ever experienced that?

I am very self-critical when I am trying to let go of a thought, emotion, or resentment, but it keeps coming back. I think, "What is wrong with me?" My community can remind me to go easier on myself, to treat myself more kindly and with more compassion. The group can guide me to self-forgiveness.

A group for moms can help you see that you are a good mother, even though you fed your kids ice cream for dinner last night. Insight from other moms allows you to forgive yourself and move on. Members of your professional community can give perspective to the times you messed up at work, knowing that none of us is perfect. By listening and offering practical advice that helps you move forward, they can help you stop the endless cycle of remembering your mistakes.

Another common criticism is the "I'm not good enough" syndrome. This idea is deep-rooted in many women. Community will have a mantra for you: "I am good enough. I am worthy. I am capable."

> "There's no prerequisites to worthiness. You're born worthy, and I think that's a message a lot of women need to hear."
> — Viola Davis

Resistance to change seems ingrained in many of us and holds us back from making progress. We don't know what's around the corner, but we know the familiar past. Fear of the unknown holds us back when we don't have a clear picture of the path forward, or when we are at a juncture but don't have the answers. Our beliefs limit us. By sharing similar experiences, community can help eliminate the fear of the unknown and the anxiety it feeds.

Feeling overwhelmed seems like standing in front of a brick wall. It may be hard to function and feels all-consuming. The to-do list seems too long. Too many stressors allow anxiety, fear, or anger to take over. Your community can remind you to take a deep breath and can help break your stressors down to smaller pieces, identifying what is controllable and what isn't. They remind you that you are not alone.

For example, if you are in a situation where you need to become a caregiver for a family member, you might feel overwhelmed and wonder how to get started and what to do. A group of women caregivers can help you break down the overall goal (to be a successful caregiver) into smaller steps. Some of the tasks might be: connect with the person's doctors; network with other caregivers; break the day into pieces, like morning, afternoon, and night, and define the needs for each time period; list the activities that require care, such as meals, rest/sleep, medications, bathing, dressing, hygiene, and socializing; and determine if you will need outside professional help for any of these items. Breaking down your responsibilities into smaller pieces will help you feel less overwhelmed.

Getting stuck feels like you can't move forward. You fear that something is not right, and don't have a path defined or a plan of how to move forward. You don't know what to do next. Feeling supported and encouraged by your community can help reduce your feelings of being stuck. You know you don't have to go through it alone. You can authentically express your fears and make the best decisions you can with the information you have. Having the environment where you can be yourself without judgment overcomes your uncertainty.

> "In anxiety-provoking situations, many women feel unable to act. They find themselves at a loss to come up with an effective response, or any response at all."
> — Stanlee Phelps and Nancy Austin

The power of community is expressed in many ways. Knowing the connection to others is available will help you find the right community and create the life energy that moves you in a positive direction. You can develop the emotional foundation you want in order to feel more confident and at ease in your life.

---

[i] http://www.sirc.org/publik/girl_talk.shtml

Chapter 2:
Finding Your Community

A simple definition of women in community is a group of close-knit women providing support for one another. Your tribe is defined as a list of women you can contact individually when you need support. This group of women may or may not know each other. A friend is someone with whom you have a close relationship. Would you say a friend could be part of your tribe or community? Do you feel alone or by yourself?

When I see women in community, I see ease, confidence, companionship, and familiarity. I want to live with more ease and confidence. I want to reduce feelings of stress and anxiety, which may come from many sources.

Safety Net

Listen to the story of my client, Katie. I am re-telling her story as she told it to me. I could see that the sparkle in her blue eyes had dimmed.

I woke up in a really bad mood. I have no idea why, but I did. The feeling was built in, and I have no way of letting it go. I'm leaving an old intimate relationship behind, one that doesn't serve me anymore. One that feels toxic, negative. I can feel that bad energy weigh me down. That may be why I am so irritable.

Leaving a relationship is difficult work for me. Hanging out in limbo here isn't helping. First, I consider how I will feel after the final separation. Am I making the right choice? Second, I don't want to cause my partner undo harm or hurt. Maybe I don't want the conflict. We don't mesh anymore; we are growing in different directions as we move forward in life.

I worry about mundane things, like what I will take with me. How will I get everything packed? Will I have enough resources when I go? Did I throw out or give away something I wish I hadn't?

My thoughts jump around to the bigger picture. Where will I live? Will I move away or stay near? What's left for me in this place? Another big question is about finances. How much money do I need to live alone? Will I have enough to live comfortably?

My anxiety and uncertainty are caused by this untold story of mine. I can't live a positive, healthy life in my current situation, but I wonder about the unknown. I can't ask questions I don't know to ask.

I am certain about my decision to move on. Sometimes there really are differences between people that can't be resolved. I wish things were different, but they aren't. I feel like I am the only one changing. I know I can't control anyone else. I will feel a loss for the good times I am leaving behind. I can change, learn, and grow.

I have been combating my stress with every tool in my box. I feel like an outsider, like I don't fit into this life anymore. My therapist has been working with me for several months now. Thankfully, she agrees that I need to leave when I'm ready.

Sitting still in meditation feels good, although sometimes my thoughts get the better of me. Slowly, my thoughts are calming down a bit. I can re-direct them to think about later. Once in a while, an enlightening thought comes my way, or I am reminded to pay attention to a certain detail, like paying a bill.

Exercise? I try strength training and jogging a few times a week. Although taking action feels good, it feels more like a chore. I practice yoga and take care not to judge myself by focusing on my breath and following one instruction at a time. Sometimes I realize that time has passed unexpectedly, like when I drive to a destination and don't remember getting there!

My doctor prescribed an anti-depressant just to take the edge off. I don't know what's working for me, but I don't seem to be feeling worse.

You could call it prayer. I ask to be the best person I can be – to be helpful and useful. I want to make the best decisions I can, and to take the next right action.

I would describe myself as the client who is doing all the right things to try to deal with stress and anxiety. I feel a void and that something is off, but I don't know what else to try. Do you ever feel that way?

Unease occurs when you leave an old phase of life, such as a relationship that no longer works. You don't know what entering the next phase looks like. You may be trying to figure out who you are when you are not in that relationship. You are wide open for new emotions, actions, and behavior because the old habits and skills no longer work.

Does it seem like Katie has someone to turn to for support? She seems fairly alone; she no longer has a relationship with her partner, and she is looking for direction. She doesn't realize that she needs a community to support her.

Katie may have a tribe or a list of friends or contacts that she could individually call. These friends may or may not know each other. Katie could call a friend on her contact list and hope her friend has helpful and encouraging words. How many times does she want to re-tell her story?

Women Supporting Women:
Redefining Friendship, Tribe, and Community

What's the difference between a set of friends who aren't connected to each other, and a community?

Think of a set of friends as a hub and spokes. As the hub, you can reach out to any individual friend (spoke) and get support. You have to pick which friend you reach for in that situation – and then hope they're available.

A community, on the other hand, is a group of women who share a commonality. It doesn't matter if the community is a card-playing club, a parenting group, a business mastermind, or a church group. The women have at least one thing in common – the binding element of the group. Because of the shared bonds of the group, you can know that you're supported from many different people, not just with a one-on-one friendship.

For a tribe, is there group synergy? Would you rather have a group of women to relate to so you could have support from several different points of view?

What do you think Katie would benefit from the most? She is dealing with stress, anxiety, and uncertainty stemming from the end of her relationship and the status of her circumstances. She thinks getting rid of the stress, anxiety, and uncertainty is the answer. Community would give Katie a sense of belonging. It would provide a safety net to fall back on, to get strength and courage from so she could find confidence to move forward and find ease in her life.

Do you have a friend or a tribe of friends in your life? How would you count on them for support if you were in a situation like Katie's? Do you have a community that would meet your needs if you were leaving a relationship? You may already have a group of close-knit women in other areas of your life, such as work, parenting, gardening, or meditation. If you do, does that group fill the void caused by your current situation?

Having a community of women to back you up provides a different perspective, encouragement, and a safety net for your choices and emotions. They can help you be your authentic self by accepting you without judgment. You will feel free to express yourself openly. These women will tell you that, in the end, everything will be okay. Moving toward growth and change takes courage, and your group helps you be confident to move in a positive direction. The power of community meets you where you are, understands where you want to go, and helps direct you to get there.

> "Female friendships that work are relationships in which women help each other belong to themselves."
> — Louise Bernikow

Chapter 3:
The Community for You

I got into a personal conversation about relationships with a young woman, Brittany, while getting a manicure at a local hair salon. Brittany is petite; I felt like I towered over her. She is attractive, with long dark hair, and she looks younger than her thirty years. She noticed me checking out her nails, which were bitten down to the quick.

Curious because a few people in my life have a similar habit, I asked her why she thought she bit her nails. She replied that it was because of stress from her relationship with her ex-boyfriend. I asked for more details and was surprised when she was so forthcoming. She told me that her ex was abusive to her, and that she always felt so small and insignificant that she couldn't get away. She felt helpless, and she nervously bit her nails from the stress. Because of her stature, she already seemed frail to me. I pictured her in that situation, which lasted several months.

As she continued her story, she shared that she started following an Instagram account that caught her attention. That account led her to another one, and after several other social media connections, she came across a women's website about narcissism. She read the comments from the online community about narcissism and recognized that many of the characteristics described were similar to her boyfriend's behavior. Everything was all about him. Brittany put a name to her problem and knew she needed to get out of her situation. She packed her things and moved into her brother's apartment.

Although she is now safe, she frequently jumps back emotionally to where she was in the relationship, and habitually bites her nails. Brittany is encouraged about breaking the habit because the nails on her little fingers are beginning to grow back.

In this case, belonging to a digital forum gave Brittany the information and courage to move forward and save herself from an unhealthy relationship. A digital forum definitely has its place in community interaction. It is a clear path if you need support or information right away. Looking online is practical and not emotional. If you find what you want, you can usually click and join. Digital community is better than no community. An online community may be a good place to start because it is convenient and the purpose or topic you need to explore may be readily available.

But I think having a face-to-face community versus a digital community is important. In today's society, most of us seem to hide behind a screen of some sort or another. Sometimes it's hard to know the truth about information you get online, and who you are actually communicating with. I feel like looking someone in the eyes, hearing their tone of voice, and seeing their body language plays a large role in interacting and connecting, and in establishing an authentic, truthful, and open relationship. In-person communication also allows other members of the community to participate in the conversation. This creates interaction with many people instead of just a friend or two.

Brittany used digital community to first identify her problem, and then for courage to leave her unhealthy environment. She has since joined an in-person community originally formed from acquaintances at work. Her current community is women she chooses to share her story with. She gets feedback and hears about similar experiences from them. For courage, Brittany used the mantra, "I am good enough. I am worthy of respect."

Does something in your life feel wrong, but you can't put your finger on it? That's okay. You're doing the best you can to figure out your uncertainty. Is there a group or community available to you to support your questions? Would you feel comfortable with an online community?

Do you have an area of your life that needs a community of women to help you move forward? The first thought that comes to my mind from this story is, "Make sure you are safe." You may need a community to help you recognize that your situation needs changing, like Brittany did. She didn't even know she needed community until she found the online forum. Your community can help you define what feels wrong to you. You can find confidence to make a change if you have a group that supports you. By connecting with other women for a specific purpose, you can keep yourself moving forward in a positive direction.

Who to Surround Yourself With

My friend, Pam, shared her story with me about time gone by, as she questioned whether she spent it wisely or not.

In the mirror, Pam saw an attractive, middle-aged woman with bright green eyes and blond highlighted hair. Thinking about her marriage, she recognized she wasn't happy. She, and her marriage, felt old. Pam and her husband questioned whether they still loved each other and what their options might be. They didn't have fun or smile much anymore. Conversations strung out into conflicts. They were like roommates living in the same house.

She spent her married years at home a lot, planning her life around her husband's schedule. They didn't do much together and rarely had exciting plans, but Pam thought that was what her role as a wife was. Deep down, she wondered if her husband was controlling her and wanted her to be available at his whim. What would happen if she had her own life outside of her marriage?

In a moment of clarity, Pam realized she was set up for disaster. Her marriage wasn't working, and she was isolated from other women because her world revolved around one person. One person – even a husband – could not meet all of her needs. She realized that one person could not meet all of anyone's needs. She wasn't sure how she let that happen and didn't know how to change her current situation. So, she did what she knew. She began calling her old friends, knowing that some of them had taken different paths in life than she did, such as being career oriented or remaining single

> "If you attach yourself to one person, you ultimately end up having an unhealthy relationship."
> – Shirley MacLaine

Pam wanted some support and interaction, so she confided her experience to some of her old friends. As she communicated with the individuals on her contact list, Pam realized there was a difference between a friend and just someone with whom she had a history. One person she contacted was only interested in gossiping about the juicy details. Another woman acted like Pam had never confided in her. Pam figured out that friends could be "fair weather" or casual, and she needed to weed out those people and find positive women to surround herself with. She learned a hard lesson that the "friends" you think you can trust may not be the friends you think they are. She was surprised by who actually stood by her to help. Reconnecting with old friends was uplifting, but she didn't feel like it gave her the meaningful interaction she needed.

Pam invited her "real" friends to a gathering to introduce them to each other. The women seemed to engage with one another naturally and were excited to talk about meeting together again. One of her friends invited another woman who she thought would enjoy belonging to the group. The group regularly met monthly. If someone suggested an additional activity, like going to a movie, cooking a special meal, or camping, each member could opt-in if she wanted to participate.

Community supported Pam in ways that individual friends could not. The members of the community that Pam brought together could all support each other by exchanging experiences, thoughts, and ideas. With her new community, Pam was able to connect and feel like she belonged and had a support network to rely on. She was honest about her feelings and felt like she could be her authentic self. She talked about the truth of her marriage and the uncertainty surrounding her next steps without being self-conscious or afraid of judgment. They helped her see the positive when she questioned her past decisions and helped her feel confident about the choices she would need to make in the future.

Women Supporting Women:
Redefining Friendship, Tribe, and Community

When another woman in the group had issues at home with teenagers, Pam was able to provide support based on her experiences while raising two teenaged boys. Being able to give as well as take helped Pam with her confidence.

Pam created a void in her life by isolating herself. She didn't recognize the need for community and used one person to take the place of many. Once she filled that void with her community, she had support and direction for moving forward.

How would you know if you were isolating yourself? What signs or symptoms would be red flags for you? Do you have a community that you could reach out to if you found yourself feeling isolated? You may feel the urge to expand your tribe or reconnect with friends from the past, forming a community.

Choose carefully who you want in your community to surround you. Some people may be toxic to a group by needing most of the attention, or by stirring the pot rather than providing support. Pam thought she knew who she could count on but learned that not everyone had her best interests at heart. Trust takes time, interaction, and observation. Being honest with yourself about how people impact your life is a good lesson to learn.

If you were to get in touch with friends from the past, what do you think would happen? Pam said, "I felt disappointed and betrayed by the way some of my old friends treated me. I found no reason to surround myself with negative people, especially since I was trying to find a way to deal with my negative marriage. I was so happy to reconnect with my true friends. We grew into a community again. It's like we were never apart." Pam celebrated re-establishing a community!

Knowing you have a community to support you brings ease to your life and relieves some of the uncertainty you may feel. You will be able to energetically hold your own space or move forward when you know you are ready.

Chapter 4: What Communities Have in Common

I visited an area church one Sunday and discovered another community of women. When I mentioned the topic of women in community, two members of the church suggested I look into the group of strong women who serve on the church board. A diverse group of women sits on the board, bringing with them skills from a variety of professions and life experiences, including art, business, human resources, law, medicine, homemaking, and finance. A defining characteristic of this group is that they are interested in getting the job done, not just fixing something. For example, they engage the congregation in planning the spiritual direction of the church, instead of just changing the intention of the service. This community is proactive and contemplative. Their intention is to listen well and watch group dynamics to hear what is trying to be said. One member of the board attributed its success to their collaboration, sensitivity to interaction, complementary etiquette (saying "thank you"), and confidence.

Unlike some informal communities, the church board is a formal community with a pre-existing structure and rules. These women are nominated by the members of the church. Their three-year-long terms include succession planning. Members of the board oversee each committee in the church. There is no micromanagement, but each committee has a person on the board to contact if there are needs or questions.

By collaborating and connecting, this group of women is able to be insightful and embody the whole picture of the organization, down to individual member ideas. Their shared skills and life experiences empower them to successfully run an organization. Their intention is to extend a positive attitude, creating a positive viewpoint for members of the church.

Have you ever been a part of a community that rallies a large group of people with diverse beliefs to successfully work together? Community leaders must cooperate and ignite cooperation from the members.

This community of women shares their experiences, strengths, and hopes as a group to successfully support the church. Each member in this diverse group plays their own role, supporting such functions as fundraising, membership, spirituality, and community (social aspects of church). The community works as an entity, and the members are interdependent pieces. The members of the board have individual roles but move as one unit to lend support and strength to the whole congregation.

Have you ever been in a position that requires you to organize and resolve differences of opinion? Would you call this church board a business group? If we define a tribe as a group of women that you could contact individually, but may not have synergy as a whole, do you think these women are also in each other's tribe? In this story, they work together to extend the spiritual experience of the church.

> "One of the marvelous things about community is that it enables us to welcome and help people in a way we couldn't as individuals."
> — Jean Vanier

Community Members Share Common Experiences

A community looks like a group of close-knit women providing support for one another. Women often share experiences to empower each other to successfully move forward in life, leaving behind the old and entering the new. They are like-minded people, but may not have the same experiences, which leaves them space to fill each other's cup. We all have strengths and weaknesses. We all have something to learn from each other. We all have something to give each other.

My friend, Cari, is short and has shoulder length, dirty-blond hair. Before becoming a mom, she was an elementary school teacher in the local district. She definitely has opinions about how life should be. Her husband traveled a lot, working in the greeting card business. Cari told me her story.

She was a new mom of a two-month-old baby girl, and her pediatrician recommended attending a workshop at the hospital for first-time new mothers to help her figure out how to care for the baby as well as herself. Cari didn't want to go because she felt she could figure out for herself whatever came her way. She was used to going it alone.

The workshop was held on a freezing-cold, Midwest winter day. Now came her first struggle: she needed to make sure the baby was dressed warmly, figure out how to fit the fully-bundled baby safely into her car seat, and keep her from crying. The drive across town to the hospital seemed to take forever, even though it was only a few miles.

Her next struggle came with figuring out how to cover and safely transport the baby from the parking lot to the building. Cari's frustration rose as she got her daughter into the stroller, covered the baby's head loosely with a blanket to shield her face from the wind, and pushed the stroller into the building. Cari couldn't imagine that this trip would be worth the effort in getting there.

She walked through the door to the hospital conference room, pushing her two-month-old baby in the stroller. Because she didn't want to be there, she had a defiant glare on her face as she glanced at each woman in the room. But her face softened as she found a seat.

Cari told me, "I didn't want to be at that meeting. I didn't want anyone telling me what to do. I knew I could handle whatever came my way. Then I looked at the other six new moms in the room with their babies, and suddenly knew I was in the right place."

When the meeting ended, the women, including Cari, established a playgroup that met every week, rotating between houses. They knew that it was easy to get isolated by staying at home during winters in the Midwest.

The group formed for moms to support each other and to share their knowledge and experiences, and for their babies to interact when they were big enough to move around. They had others to call on if they had questions: "Which pediatrician do you use?" "What do you do for a fever?" "How are you handling teething?" "At what age do they crawl?"

They learned from sharing each other's experiences and ideas. This community celebrated many wins, too. "She sat up for the first time!" "He's crawling now." "Her first tooth poked through last Thursday!"

Cari's story shows that community forms around similar experiences and support, knowing that you don't have to go it alone. At some point, you may realize that you need other communities in your life that address different areas, such as business, fitness, or health. Not everyone in these groups understands what being a new mom is like.

If you were Cari, what would you do if you had a question about being a new mom that you didn't know the answer to? Would you go through your phone's contact list to identify someone who had a child similar in age to yours? What would you do if that person didn't answer the phone? What would be your next move if you couldn't find somebody who had experiences you could draw from? (For the sake of this example, we're assuming that if the question was urgent, you could call 911 or your pediatrician!)

Before joining this community, Cari would have to hope that she personally knew another mom who would have the real-life experience and advice that she needed. But as a member of her new mom community, Cari could wait until the next meeting, present the question to the group, and get more than one response. Maybe other moms would help her realize questions that she didn't even know to ask.

That's powerful! That's the power of community and how it works to support women in their growth – as moms and as people.

What about you? Maybe you're blessed to have an endless list of contacts in your phone so that no matter what your question, no matter the time of day, no matter the date on the calendar, you could find somebody.

Women Supporting Women:
Redefining Friendship, Tribe, and Community

Most of us aren't like that. We have a few close friends, but not an endless contact list. Being a member of a community means you have many more people to reach out to for help and support, no matter what transitions you experience in your life.

When you don't have a community that can support you – to make you feel connected and understood, and to have your questions addressed – then you're left all by yourself. And that's a lonely place to be.

Communities Support Transitions

Paula's son, Chris, is taller and stronger than her. His brown hair and big blue eyes add to his good looks. They had just driven two hours in her Toyota 4-Runner; it was packed to the roof with boxes, bins, and miscellaneous articles from his bedroom. Chris picked up a large, heavy-looking box from the back of the car and carried it down the sidewalk, up the front stairs, and into the long brown building. Then he trudged up three flights of stairs to the fourth floor, the top floor. The building was old, smelled of stale beer, and had no elevator. He was moving into his first college dorm.

As Paula watched him, she said to herself, "I'm not going to cry. I'm not going to cry." She was filled with anxiety over his leaving – concerned that he was happy and making the right choices, and not sure who she was without him.

Paula lifted a plastic bin out of the car and began the long trek up to the fourth floor. Moving was a workout; they were breaking a sweat and breathing hard. They met another student, Jason, who had already moved into the room across the hall. Somehow, knowing that Chris knew someone else there made Paula feel lighter.

As they moved his belongings to his room, the car got emptier and his small dorm room got fuller. Paula realized the time to say goodbye was getting closer. "I'm not going to cry in front of him. I'm not going to cry in front of him." She knew that this was the next natural step in his life. Even so, sadness over the separation overrode the understanding that he was growing up and needed to move on.

After they carried the last load up the stairs, they arranged the boxes, bins, computer, room-sized refrigerator, and personal items so that he had room to move around the small living space while he unpacked and organized himself.

Paula could feel her face pucker up and her throat tighten. Tears started to spring up in her eyes. Trying to hold them back, she said to herself, "I'm not going to cry until I turn around and start walking away. I'm not going to cry until I turn around and start walking away." Intellectually, she knew some things would be easier for both of them when they weren't directly involved in each other's daily lives. Emotionally, that didn't matter.

They hugged, said "I love you," and then goodbye. She turned around and walked away. Who knew sending a child off to college would be so hard? She knew the day was coming but wasn't prepared for the feelings of loss and separation. Tears rolled down her cheeks. She cried off and on the whole two-hour ride home, and randomly cried for the next four days.

Paula realized she had lost touch with parents of kids Chris's age, and wondered how they fared when their children left for college. She wished the moms still got together and stayed in contact with each other.

As a mom, you might feel the sorrow for time gone by and the end of childhood but understand intellectually that growing up is necessary and liberating for the young adult. Of course, you may be ready for your child to leave home, but worry if your child is happy, attending classes, and doing homework.

What could Paula have done to relieve some of her anxiety and uncertainty? She thought about thumbing through his high school yearbook to see if she recognized anyone. Then she could try to contact the mom who belonged to that person. She could have just asked Chris which of his friends were going to college.

Contacting several moms who had college-bound children and inviting them to meet for coffee would be a start. Paula began by talking to the few moms she knew who were in a similar situation and asked them if they knew other women whose kids were moving out. She hoped for a snowball effect, for the small group to quickly grow in number. Many women felt relieved to get in touch with people who were having a similar experience. But they didn't recognize the need for community until Paula asked them.

Not only does community help with immediate needs, but it also energetically holds women together to address challenges that unexpectedly arise and transitions we aren't aware of yet. For example, Paula soon had another question. Chris was her first child to leave home. Would she feel differently when the next child, her daughter, left? She was excited to ask her new community the question.

What has come up unexpectedly in your life that you wish you had a community for? You may find you need community for an area of your life that you don't have covered yet.

> "Sometimes the transition from being in control of your life to having absolutely no control is swift, but other times it is so gradual that you wonder exactly when it truly began."
> — Mickey Rooney

Paula needed a group of women to reassure her to let go of things that were not in her control. She could be her authentic self, being honest about her feelings because the women in the community had been through similar circumstances. They understood and did not judge her thoughts.

Women Supporting Women:
Redefining Friendship, Tribe, and Community

Community supports women with similar experiences in life – the natural transitions between one phase of life and another. Sometimes the unexpected happens and community gathers to share and to stand together.

Chapter 5:
How Communities Grow and Evolve

In 1942, after much controversy, a program was established to train women to fly for the military. WASP, Women Airforce Service Pilots, was formed because of a shortage of male military pilots in WWII. Some of the decision-making men in the government questioned whether women were capable of flying. However, women who already had a flying license and 100 hours of flying time were eligible to apply to be a WASP. 25,000 women applied for the positions; almost 1,900 were accepted; and approximately 1,100 passed the military training program. They had one thing in common – these women loved to fly!ⁱⁱ

The training for women was similar to that of men, except for combat gunnery and formation flying. They trained hard for seven months in physical and drill training, flight instruction, and aircraft mechanics, among other things. They learned to fly different aircraft, and studied subjects such as weather, navigation, and technical information about engines. If they had any down time at night, they were known to relax and socialize. They were called the Avenger Girls because their rigorous training was held at Avenger Field in Sweetwater, Texas.

These women were considered civilian volunteers, even though they ferried aircraft from base to base, tested new and repaired planes, and provided target practice by pulling targets behind the planes they were flying. Can you imagine equipment malfunctions on the planes to be tested? What about a misguided shot to a target pulled behind a plane you were flying?

The program lasted only two years because at the end of the war, returning male pilots wanted the positions the women filled. The WASP program was disbanded. Thirty-eight members died during duty. The women weren't paid or even acknowledged by the military. As a group, they collected money to send their own dead home. They weren't even given transportation home after the program ended. The gender discrimination went deeper than the closure of the program. There were even allegations of sabotage to ensure the women failed at their mission.

The community of women connected and attended reunions. Mostly, the group held together because of the way they were treated by the military. They wanted to be recognized as contributors for their efforts rather than disregarded as no longer useful. They rose above adversity and wanted acknowledgement for making an impact in WWII.

In 1976, the Air Force announced that they were accepting female recruits for the first time. Because they had served in the Air Force years before, this action made the WASP pilots feel like they were being wiped from history. Being forgotten by their own military united the women to take action. In 1977, they received military status. Finally, in 2010, the surviving members of the WASPs were awarded a Congressional Gold Medal.

The WASPs formed a community for a very specific purpose – to fly planes to support the military and serve their country. After that purpose was fulfilled, the community seemed to stay together almost as self-defense, to stand up for themselves. They wanted acknowledgement for their contributions, for a job well done, and for their losses. The advent of public internet, messaging, email, and finally social media made communication between the WASP members more accessible and brought their cause to the attention of more people.

Communities take on many different shapes as needed. I was drawn to this group because I saw a picture of several women in their self-created uniforms walking across a tarmac with an airplane in the background. The determination and pride in their roles as pilots showed through in their stride, posture, and faces. They had a definite look of confidence and comradery. This story shows that communities may organize for a specific purpose, and through no fault of their own, evolve into another form.

Have you ever felt disregarded? What did you do to find your voice? Would coming together as a group help you make a stronger stand for yourself? Standing together as a group allowed these women to ultimately get recognition for their contributions to WWII that they weren't able to get before they united. The purpose of the community you start out with may evolve to another purpose because of circumstances outside of your control.

If you have a community, do you feel confident you can gather together to solve a problem? If you don't have a community, do you think having one would help you stand up for yourself and speak your needs?

Think of the power in numbers and like-minded intention. The WASPs addressed an issue in full force and achieved their desired outcome through community. By evolving from the purpose of women piloting in WWII, the community organized as a group to gain recognition. That's a celebration! That's the power of community.

Spinoff Communities Forming Themselves

My local fitness center has been around for thirty years or so. Several years ago, a group of women connected after they signed up for the same strength class taught by a popular trainer. The trainer was known to be pretty loud and tough, but very personable and group oriented. She liked making games out of challenges. The women varied in height, size, age, and skill level. They liked completing the challenges with one another. As a group, they became stronger and more coordinated.

The trainer started an email list to keep everyone in touch with each other, sharing gym news, fitness tips, and days and times of extracurricular activities. These women rallied around the trainer and continued to take her classes. As time went on, some women from the group tried other classes and forms of exercise, such as running, biking, and yoga. They supported each other's efforts and progress in the strength class; they found ways to round out their fitness levels and decrease imbalances by becoming involved in other areas of fitness that seemed interesting.

Laurie and Kim, two members of the group, decided to start jogging. The trainer suggested they go to a forest preserve trail, jog out a half-mile, then turn around and walk back. (The forest preserve trails have mile markers.) The next day, they were to jog out a half-mile, then turn around and jog halfway back, walking the rest of the way back. The idea was to lengthen the amount of time they jogged each time they went out. Laurie was shorter than Kim and had a smaller stride, but they made it work even if Kim had to turn around and jog back to meet Laurie when she got too far ahead.

Continuing to train with this advice, they quickly increased their distance to 3.1 miles, the length of a 5K race. Laurie and Kim signed up for a 5K race, and the rest of the group went out to support them. Being cheered on by the rest of their workout group, both women finished the 5K and vowed to increase their speed for the next race. The race was an exciting event, and the rest of the community decided to pick up jogging, too. They went out on the trails and trained as a team.

Two other women, Carla and Jeanie, really liked to bike. With the enthusiasm of the group, the whole community started biking on the forest preserve trails. First, they decided what type of bikes to ride and where to buy them. As time passed in their training, they increased their time, speed, and distance. They would ride and then jog. The next time they went out, they would repeat that and ride and then jog. They also noticed that being outside was a nice way to reduce stress, exercise, and spend time together.

One of the women heard about a women's triathlon being held in the area. A triathlon is a race that starts with swimming, transitions to biking, and then ends with running. The group decided to sign up and added swimming laps at the gym pool to their training program. Race day came; none of them had ever competed in a triathlon. Before the start of the triathlon was very nerve racking, because the participants had to wait in flights to begin the swimming portion. One of the women swam alongside another one who felt unsure about her swimming capability and endurance. After the end of the swimming portion, they just saw each other in passing as they transitioned through to the biking section and then the running segment. They cheered each other to the finish line. The women all finished the race and were motivated to continue together in their fitness journey. The fitness group not only celebrated wins from races, but achieving training goals, finishing competitions, and completing another mile! Groups evolve as their members evolve. This community started out as a strength fitness class. As interests in other areas of fitness grew, the group took on the new challenges and trained in the new modalities (running, biking, swimming, and competing). These women were open-minded and willing to try new adventures. They became genuine friends and supported each other's schedules, events, and families.

Is it easier for you to do something with someone else than alone? Do you have a community that has evolved and changed as the interests of the group have changed? Individuals in your group may have grown together and expanded the purpose of your group. You may have realized that experiencing new activities with other people is more enjoyable, and you might not have tried them if you were alone. Your group can start for one purpose and become a life force that develops and evolves as the group changes.

Evolving Communities

Some communities form naturally by location, such as a neighborhood. A close-knit group of women from my old neighborhood, originally organized as a bunco group, has been in place for many years. When I moved away, I sadly left the group behind, knowing I wouldn't be as involved in their lives as I would be if I still lived in the neighborhood.

One of the women, Leslie, was a stay-at-home mom and was very surprised when her husband came home one night and told her he was divorcing her. Evidently, he had planned his strategy to get out of the marriage and was well ahead of her in terms of being prepared to get the most out of the assets they shared. He already had another place to stay and accounts in his own name. Feeling hurt and betrayed, she knew she needed to make sure their three children were cared for in the best way possible. The bunco community listened to her vent, vetted her ideas about what to do in the future, and helped her when she needed a reality check.

Leslie got a job teaching in an elementary school across town. She needed to sell their house and buy a smaller one. She prepared the current house for sale and put it on the market with a real estate agent. The ladies in the bunco group took turns looking at suitable houses with her as they came available on the market. Finally, an acceptable house in the same neighborhood was available at the same time that her current house got a contract. Leslie sat on the stairs of the smaller house, checking out the feel of the place to be sure she and her kids could happily live there.

On the day of the move, the women of the community and their husbands all showed up at her old house with boxes in hand. They helped her pack, go through closets, and throw things away. She hired a moving company for the bigger items, but the bunco group loaded their cars with the boxes they'd packed and drove to the new home. They unpacked, noting which room each box belonged in, cleaning silverware and dishes before putting them away in the cabinets, and hanging clothes in the closets. Leslie was able to get her family settled with the least amount of worry and disruption possible.

This community of women from bunco supported Leslie in a way that kept her sane, carried her through her divorce, and helped her successfully move in a short period of time. Even though she was hurt and angry with her soon-to-be ex-husband, she knew that all would be well for her kids and herself because she had a community holding them up during the tough times.

Leslie originally joined the group to play cards. This group was formed for recreation and friendship. But the women developed genuine friendships, and they evolved into a group of women that supported Leslie and her children when her life had an unexpected change.

> "It's astonishing in this world how things don't turn out at all the way you expect them to."
> — Agatha Christie

Women Supporting Women:
Redefining Friendship, Tribe, and Community

Leslie actively participated as a member of this bunco group from the beginning, and when her life changed, she was authentic and honest about her feelings and needs. The group was able to hold her up and support her to move forward. Helping Leslie wasn't any one person's responsibility. Being in the right community contributed to receiving support from many different individuals.

How has your life unexpectedly changed? Were you shocked? Surprised? Able to handle the outcome? Maybe you experienced loss through a change in location or employment. Your loss may have been because of a death or the end of a relationship that forced you to change or move away from a familiar lifestyle. Would the change have been easier knowing that you had backup?

Being in a community can create a positive support group that is available for the amazing life changes that unpredictably happen. Community can repair, protect, and develop as members move through different phases of life.

[ii] https://www.npr.org/2010/03/09/123773525/female-wwii-pilots-the-original-fly-girls
https://www.army.mil/women/history/pilots.html

https://www.womenshistory.org/exhibits/women-airforce-service-pilots-wasps-wwii

https://www.britannica.com/topic/Women-Airforce-Service-Pilots

Chapter 6:
How to Know if You've Outgrown Your Community

"I knew I was pregnant, but now I know I'm carrying twins! What does that mean?"

"When I told my mom, she asked me if I was kidding. I had to convince her it was real."

"I bought a pre-printed note pad with the title – Twins in the Family."

"I began to be freaked out about how much work twins would be, and how I would be able to handle two of everything. Little did I know that I had to get through the pregnancy first."

Women Supporting Women:
Redefining Friendship, Tribe, and Community

These are quotes from Sheri, when she learned that she was pregnant with twins. Here's the rest of her story:

I was definitely surprised when the doctor told me I was carrying twins. I never had any exposure to multiple births, so I felt clueless about what all it involved. I was panicked, thinking about having to do two of everything. I felt double the responsibility and wondered how I would cope.

One of my husband's work colleagues was a parent of twins. He gave my husband his wife's contact information so I could get in touch with her. When I called her, she invited me to her house to talk about my questions, like how to handle two of everything.

She told me about a group for moms of twins called DuPage Doubles. I attended one of their monthly meetings, and the group was very welcoming. They reassured me and provided information and support. Having twins made me an instant member; I felt like I belonged. I attended a few get-togethers and watched around me as younger twins were cared for and the older ones moved about to play. Moms were able to compare notes with each other and provide suggestions when someone needed advice. They celebrated their children's milestones and navigated each new phase of development. For example, when a child starts to walk, the child also needs to be watched closer because she can get to more places.

Life seemed a little chaotic. I felt stifled. The moms of twins understood what I was going through. They listened and offered reassurance, reiterating that life with twins was doable and even wonderful.

As it turns out, multiple-birth pregnancies are very risky and can be quite complicated. Because multiple-birth pregnancies were never part of my life, I never considered the consequences or knew any details. Many of the pregnancies don't last full term, and some of the complications that are well known to single pregnancies occur more often with twins. The twins group understood about high-risk pregnancies.

As I brushed my teeth one morning, blood began running down my leg. My husband took me to the emergency room, where I was admitted to the hospital. I remember that I couldn't stop shaking because I was shocked and worried about the babies. I was put on bed rest due to a condition called placenta previa.

Bed rest is a game-changer. Think about not being able to participate in life. First, I had to find someone to care for my toddler. A woman from the neighborhood came by to watch him and left him to play while she rearranged my linen closet. That wasn't going to work! I was so thankful that the moms in the twins group told me about a babysitter list at the local college. I started calling down the list of names and found a girl that sounded good and matched my schedule and needs.

Women Supporting Women:
Redefining Friendship, Tribe, and Community

She came by to meet Brian, my son. As I lay in bed, I could hear giggles from the den. I knew that the new sitter would work out and that Brian would be happy. The moms in the twins community also arranged to bring meals by the house so I wouldn't have to worry about what my son and husband would eat.

This is how it feels to have a group that understands what you are going through. Bed rest is unbelievably boring, and it robs you of acts of daily living, but the responsibilities of life still need to be taken care of.

While in the hospital, an ultrasound showed that one of the babies was considerably smaller than the other one. The difference in size was notable enough to send me to a specialist in a high-risk hospital, about an hour away, which had a neo-natal unit. My husband or his mother drove me to weekly appointments. Thirty-two weeks into the pregnancy, on my weekly visit to the hospital, the doctor only detected one heartbeat.

Yes," the doctor said. "It's a demise."

I was furious. What does "It's a demise" mean, exactly? His bedside manner was non-existent. That's not how you tell someone her baby died!

I was in the hospital for a week trying to give the other baby time to mature more, knowing that the twins group was helping with meals and the sitter was caring for Brian. The delivery was bittersweet – one baby to care for and one baby to bury.

I couldn't be part of the twins group anymore. The experience was too painful, and I felt like an outsider. I recognized that I didn't fit in and needed to move on.

Sheri felt better putting distance between her and the mothers she met in the community. She knew that the community understood her, but realized it was time to leave.

> "The greatness of a community is most accurately measured by the compassionate actions of its members."
> – Coretta Scott King

Some communities are formed for specific reasons, like the group for multiple births. If you change, and the community stays the same, it's time to leave and find a community that's right for you. This is a clear example of belonging to a community that understands you but recognizing when it no longer fits.

Do you have a community that no longer serves you, because either you or the community changed? What would you do if you needed to leave a community? Sheri could seek out a group of women that suited her current situation. She could ask the twins group if they knew of a community that wasn't for multiple births or call her doctor's office to ask about a community for new moms.

Women Supporting Women:
Redefining Friendship, Tribe, and Community

She could ask friends and neighbors or look online for a local group that would serve her needs.

If your community no longer serves you in your situation, how do you plan to move forward? You may feel alone, or that something just isn't right. You may be afraid of what the future holds. You may recognize that it is time to find another group of women who are like-minded and who are experiencing similar life events. Would belonging to a group of women who listen to your thoughts and feelings help you feel uplifted and supported?

Looking at this situation from the community's viewpoint, the community had a specific purpose – to support families of multiple births. It was not designed to evolve, change, or be all-encompassing. Sheri no longer met the purpose of the group. Sheri and the twins group both benefitted by acknowledging that a change was necessary.

Being in the right community helps both the member and the community by creating a sense of belonging and connectedness between all members as individuals, and the group as a whole. Finding the right community for your needs helps you move forward in a positive direction.

Chapter 7:
When the Community Isn't a Good Fit

One of my workout friends, Alice, is tall like me. I know her from the fitness center; she likes to swim and attend land classes. Alice was happy to retire and have more time to do things like work out and volunteer. A long-standing group of women from her neighborhood asked her to join their community, which met two times a week for two to three hours, usually for coffee. She started attending the get togethers almost out of a feeling of obligation. The women talked about topics such as local life, recipes, families, and church. They brought knitting or stitching projects to work on.

Women Supporting Women:
Redefining Friendship, Tribe, and Community

"I was so bored, I didn't know what to do," Alice said. They sent out group emails to announce each meeting, specifying the time and place. "I dreaded having to go, but I didn't want to be rude. I mean, they are nice ladies. But their interests were not for me. I needed to be productive and didn't have time for sitting and socializing that much. Thankfully, I was asked to go back to work part time and was able to use that as an excuse not to attend the meetings."

The women complained that Alice's work and volunteer activities interfered with her participation in the group. "I have so much more to contribute to life than sitting still and re-hashing common information. Eventually, they took me off of the weekly reminder email and now I am just on the special events email. But I would rather stay home and work on something at the house than go to special events."

This was clearly not the community for Alice. She didn't want to feel bad or make the group feel bad, but she needed to get out of the situation. Rather than supporting her personal growth, the group held her back. It did not meet her needs, nor did it evolve or grow to meet the needs of their newest member.

How do you know if a community is right for you? Notice the life of the community, and whether it supports your feeling of belonging. Is the group diverse enough to keep up with the changing needs of the community? Do you have confidence in the group's advice, ideas, and actions? Does the group meet your needs?

Do you belong to a club or group that you dread attending? Can you think of a circumstance in your life that does not feel good to be a part of?

Ask yourself the following questions. Do I look forward to the meetings? Am I contributing to others and getting my needs met? Do I have energy and excitement after we meet?

Your answers can help direct you about your future in the group. You may decide to stay but change your role within the group; for example, you become the mentor instead of the mentee. Or, you may realize that you need to move on.

The right community will provide an energetic lift for you, helping you to grow in a positive direction. You will want to belong, and you will be excited about the possibilities for growth.

If the purpose of the group isn't one that supports your life, it's time to move on. You are always in control. You can opt out if the community no longer meets your needs.

> "Women can be powerful, graceful, and complex, with the ability to make any choice they desire."
> — Jessica Chastain

Chapter 8:
Starting a New Community

Rita heard a knock on her front door, even though she wasn't expecting anyone to come over. She glanced through the peephole and saw a young woman standing outside the door. Taking a chance, Rita decided to open the door even though she did not know the person on the other side.

The woman introduced herself as Marie, a neighbor from across the street. She explained that she really wanted to connect to other single women and was planning a dinner party for the single women in the neighborhood. Through knocking on doors, she had met three single women in a row across the street, one two doors down, and another at the end of the road.

This seemed like an interesting idea to Rita; everyone who was invited knew at least one other person on the invitation list. Marie opened up her house to virtual strangers who lived in her neighborhood. The dinner party turned out to be great fun and evolved into a monthly event sponsored by different members of the group. There was no ulterior motive to establishing this community other than wanting single, female friends. They had each other's backs; they asked each other for help. There was always a volunteer from the group if someone needed the dog walked or the trash carried to the curb. The women not only connected, they seemed to mesh with one another.

Finding a community you fit into may not be easy. Some communities may come together naturally through groups like neighborhoods, work, and life events. You may have to start one of your own by adding to your tribe of one. Marie started her singles group by knocking on doors. She took a chance.

> I feel there is something unexplored about woman that only a woman can explore.
> – Georgia O'Keeffe

When you are looking for a community or feel the need to start one, listen around you to hear of similar situations to find women you resonate with. Being open, filling the void with kind actions, being helpful, smiling, listening,

Women Supporting Women:
Redefining Friendship, Tribe, and Community

and putting yourself in social situations are a few of the ways to start or find community. You can reach out to women you know, accept new women into your circle, and determine who shares a common interest or bond with you. If you typically are quiet or introverted, you may have to step out of your comfort zone to form or learn about community. Let other women know that you are looking for a community.

Do you wish you had a group of women who were in a similar place in their lives with similar experiences? Marie purposely formed a group to meet the needs of single women. Maybe you already belong to a group that doesn't suit your purpose, and you understand that you have a different void to fill and want to create a community that serves you, like Marie did. You may have to form your own community if you don't find one that fits your needs.

Chapter 9:
Joining a Community

Are you ready to join a community? Here are some questions to consider.

Does the purpose of the community resonate with your beliefs and values? The community should match your needs at the time. When your needs and the community's purpose line up, you have value to contribute to the group. But a mismatch in beliefs and values will create tension.

For example, if you are a down-to-earth person and are very comfortable in jeans, joining a group of put-together, fashionista women might not be comfortable. You're not judging either set of beliefs but lining up with who you are is important to you and your community.

Another example is if the community goes for high visibility, and you are a more laid back, behind-the-scenes type of person. In that case, neither you nor the community will be comfortable with your interaction.

In Alice's story, she understood that her beliefs and those of the group were different. Rather than socialize several hours a week, she wanted to volunteer, be productive, and work part time.

Can you align your actions and values within the purpose of the community? You should feel a connection and know you are in the right place. You want community members to act in a way that you are comfortable with and find meaningful. Not that everyone needs to be homogenous; but for example, you might want to hike and camp for the enjoyment of nature and the sense of spirituality you get from it, while another person might want to hike and camp to get away from everyday life and party for a while. The purpose of the community and the reality of the community should be in alignment with your values and be acceptable to you.

Does the community speak to your personality and style? For example, if you are a more structured or black-and-white person, you may be uncomfortable with a community run in an ambiguous, haphazard, or unorganized manner. A community without leadership or a set of rules may be awkward for you. On the other hand, your goal may be to step out of your comfort zone and learn from someone who does not organize life the same way you do. In that case, joining a community that is run differently than you are used to could be a good learning experience. Growth happens from positive as well as negative perspectives.

Do you feel like you are included and belong? If you are joining an already-established community, there is a process of getting to know each other. You may not feel a sense of belonging from day one, but unless the community feels overtly unwelcoming, stick with the process long enough to realize if it's a good fit. Social skills allow the rapport to be built.

This is true for starting a new community as well. The women in the single women group that Marie started didn't all know each other but seemed to naturally bond with each other. When Sheri joined the twins group, she was included, but she took her time getting to know some of the moms. She attended group gatherings to get the feel of the women, even though she was panicked about having twins – which was the purpose of the group.

Are you in agreement with any informal or formal guidelines established by the group? Most communities have spoken or unspoken rules or guidelines. Feel free to ask what they are. The guidelines may be as simple as: the group meets at someone's house each month; or, each person will host a meeting at their house every eight weeks; or, clean up after yourself before you leave. In the church board example, each person was voted into position and had a designated role assigned to them to support specific committees, the church as a whole, and the needs of individual members. The group had term limits and a succession plan to follow. In this case, is the amount of responsibility right for you? Could you honor the length of the commitment?

Are the meetings easily accessible for you? The where, when, and how of a community meeting is integral to the function of the group. For example, if the meeting is an hour away, do the benefits you get from attending the meeting outweigh the time in the car? If you are not a night person, will you be happy going to a night meeting? If you work throughout the day, would a lunch time meeting work with your schedule? You have permission not to join the community because you can't get there!

Is there an agreement of confidentiality? Confidentiality may vary with the purpose of the community. A bunco group may not value confidentiality as much as a group that supports women going through divorce. What do you think? I believe that both formal and informal meetings should have some safeguards in place so that you have a safe space to be your authentic self without worrying if you will see yourself on social media the next day. You should feel confident that what you say or how you feel will be held privately and not passed around. In Pam's story, she realized that a woman she confided in gossiped about her to other people. She knew she didn't need that woman in her life.

Thinking back to purpose, does the community support you where you are, and know where you want to go? Are the members able to help you get there? The group of empty nesters came together to support each other when their children left for college. Cari turned to her group of new moms with questions about motherhood and life with infants. Both of these communities supported women transitioning through natural phases of life.

Is there a cost to be part of the community? If so, is joining worth the cost? You may want to learn what the money is used for, and if the fee is a one-time contribution or a recurring charge. Membership in the WASP group of female WWII pilots unofficially cost a lot! They had to pay for their own training and piloting licenses, their transportation to and from working in the service, and even to transport back home their colleagues who died during active duty. Those expenses may not feel like dues, charges, or fees; but the women definitely paid a high price for belonging to the group.

What benefits do you receive as part of the community? Benefits may include direction, inspiration, insight, confidence, support, calmness, and higher self-esteem. You want to feel supported in celebrations, learning, and problem solving. You will be bringing balance to parts of your life that are shifting. Evaluate your needs and decide if the positive feelings you take away are greater than any negative feelings you may have. You want to use the community in the way that meets your needs. In the story of the fitness workout group, the women practiced and participated together. They encouraged and celebrated each other as they met their fitness goals and completed various competitions and challenges.

Is there opportunity for growth? How can you contribute to the community? Are you willing to be an active participant? A community isn't a separate entity.

Women Supporting Women:
Redefining Friendship, Tribe, and Community

You get to be a part of it. A community isn't a "would be nice-to-have" thing in your life. You have value, and your experiences can help other women move forward in a positive manner. This requires a time commitment on your part. It also requires putting yourself out there. You want to get out of the community what you put into it. You can ask yourself, "Is this a great community for me, and can I contribute to making it great?"

You want to find purpose, relief, support, and confidence in yourself and the group. The community knows where you want to be and is willing to help you get there. You want to feel like you are moving forward in a positive direction, and that the community supports that move. Decide how you want to use the community and ensure that you have a match! For example, if you want to learn, make sure you will be learning. If you think about Brittany and the narcissist boyfriend, she inadvertently found the right community to support her and encourage her to move out of an unhealthy relationship. She was relieved to know she wasn't alone, and that there was a name for her boyfriend's problem – and it wasn't her! She identified her need to get away from her relationship with a narcissist, and she found the information, courage, and support to take action.

Decide how you can contribute to the community to add value to other women's lives. In Brittany's example, members of the community contributed enough information and shared enough experiences with the group that she was able to make a connection and help herself be safe.

What don't you want?

Think in terms of gossip, toxicity, controlling and attention-seeking behavior, and drama.

How do you feel about those issues? Can you think of other things that would not be good for you?

> "Get rid of the backstabbers – surround yourself only with people who will lift you higher."
> – Oprah Winfrey

Are you interested in the group and its purpose? Remember Alice? She was bored with the socialization of her group and would rather volunteer, work, or do a project at home.

Do you leave the meetings feeling energized or exhausted?

If the health of the community is in any way toxic to you, it's okay to leave. Some examples are: if the community acts like you aren't valuable if you don't belong, and if the community has an "if you win, I lose" attitude.

Do you feel like you need to explain yourself or justify your actions? Being a member of a community isn't about being controlled or judged. You need to feel free to be who you are.

What to expect when joining a community

If you are starting a community, you and the initial members can decide how it will be organized and run until such a time that something different seems to work better or other ideas are put into place.

For example, the empty-nest moms decided to meet at a coffee shop once a week, each person paying for their own refreshment. If a member couldn't come, the group expected them to let another member know beforehand. Early on in the development of the group, a group email was put together. One member volunteered for a month to send out weekly reminder emails of the meeting, and members could respond if they weren't coming. The group was very informal but recognized if members didn't attend. They appreciated participation. Members cared about members.

The group for new moms started with the intention of meeting at someone's house each week. The rotation of meeting place was decided ahead of time. The hostess provided drinks and snacks for the adults. Each mom brought drinks and snacks for their own baby. Each person was responsible for cleaning up after herself before leaving. This arrangement was also informal and casual. The new mom community noticed if members were not there and wanted them to check in if they would not attend. The group was concerned if there was an issue, like someone being sick or traveling.

The intention with these two communities was for each woman to decide for herself if the purpose of the community honored her needs. Group decisions worked when choices needed to be made, and no one person was "in charge." The groups met for their intended purpose. If someone suggested an event in addition to the scheduled meetings, each member could decide if she wanted to attend.

Whether you are starting a group or joining one that already exists, you may all come in as strangers, and get to know each other as the community develops. You may make new friends; some members might bond closer than others. Someone you are not entirely close to may be the right person with the right answers to your questions! You may be the right person to provide input to someone who needs your insight.

Communities with more formal structures could include business masterminds, networking groups, cooking classes, and various not-for-profit clubs. These groups may be organized with dues and standard operating procedures. You need to decide what level of seriousness, accountability, or degree of structure would serve you. You are the right person to decide what environment will meet your interests and needs most.

How many communities do you want to belong to? If the community fits your needs and fills you up without anyone taking you down, the community can serve its purpose. You can decide if you feel great being a member or choose to move on. You may not have the time or the energy to participate in several communities. The number is up to you. Community has a powerful positive impact on your life. You choose which ones to belong to.

Once you join a community, you will have the opportunity to interact with other members and decide where you want to fit into the overall framework of the group.

> "As women, we may not be a minority, but there is a bond that we all share. It is not a bond of geography. Or religion. Or culture. It is a bond of shared experience – experiences that only women go through and struggles that only women face."
> — Amal Clooney

Chapter 10:
The Life of a Community

The life of a community includes the interactions of members within the community. My client, Joan, had several interesting insights about a community she belonged to. Joan loves to dance and has an easy smile. She attended several group dance classes, loved one instructor in particular, and personally knew several people in the class.

A couple of years ago, a few friends from the dance class decided to form a book club as a way to meet and socialize outside of class time. They set up the initial guidelines. They met every other month at someone's house. The hostess chose the book for the next meeting. The originators of the group tracked the meeting location, date, time, and book on a spreadsheet. They also decided to limit the size of the group to twelve members. They felt they couldn't include everyone from dance class, because the group would be too big to meet at a home, and they would have difficulty sharing everyone's ideas.

Joan personally knew a few of the women who joined the book club, but only knew the rest from seeing them in the dance class. Here are some of her observations: "The book club gave me the chance to get to know some of the women I didn't know to begin with. Also, I realized I had made assumptions or formed opinions about some of the women which turned out to be wrong. Getting to know them better through the community made me realize they weren't who I thought they were, and we actually became good friends."

"Some of the people who joined the book club weren't even big readers," Joan said. "They joined for the social aspect of the group. So, they really liked to be hostess so they could choose the next book to read."

This community had rules, like the size of the group, the meeting place and date, who chose the book to read, and how they tracked the meetings. The group also had expectations of each member, such as: read the book if you want to be part of the discussion; don't gossip about each other; and socialize after the discussion.

In reality, this is an example of one community forming another community. The initial qualification for joining was being part of the dance class. The members of the class enjoyed themselves so much that they wanted to have a purpose to meet outside of class. Each person had a say in discussing the book, though not everyone liked the book chosen. The community time also included recreation and socialization.

Members of the book club represented a diverse group of people. They were all a little different from each other, with a wide variety of opinions. Joan also noted, "Talking about someone in the community to another member didn't work out well." Each person may perceive what they see or hear differently than someone else. For example, if a member spent discussion time summarizing the book for someone who did not read it, one person might feel that was a waste of time, while another person might feel that she was being talked down to.

Interactions between people in the community may not always be agreeable or be what you perceive them to be. As a participant in the group, try to understand before being understood. You may need to keep your perceptions of other members to yourself until you know more about the group dynamics. You will need to have an accepting attitude towards women who may feel differently than you do.

The example of the book club brings to mind personal interactions between people in a community. Gossip is about revealing something personal or spreading a rumor about a person. Gossip and rumors are not verified information, and they can sometimes be damaging to the person being talked about. Someone may gossip to build a social bond with someone else, thinking that sharing something negative is more intimate than sharing something positive. Sometimes, gossip is repeated as fact and can wind up hurting people. A person may gossip to feel better about themselves, revealing something negative about that person's character. Gossip isn't okay in a community (or anywhere), so if you hear it, try to catch yourself before becoming involved in the conversation. You can change the subject or try problem solving instead of stirring the pot.

Communities are formed in many different ways and include interactions between the members. The life of the community has its own character based on the actions of the members. Some communities have members transitioning in or out. Your interactions in the community may shift based on the fabric of the membership. The character of the community may change based on the continuity of the membership.

Chapter II:
Transient Communities

Another form of community I'd like to explore is the idea of a temporary community. Not that all other communities are permanent, but that some communities are purposely formed for a specific reason, for a specific amount of time. If you consider classes or courses, not all classes become communities. A shorter-term class – one that meets once a week for six weeks, for example – would not likely form community. Likewise, participants in a weekend workshop may not form a community, as the members do not invest enough time in the group. They don't have enough skin in the game. Bonds of friendship may not form as easily in a shorter-term,

Women Supporting Women:
Redefining Friendship, Tribe, and Community

transient community because of limitations in time, commitment, and interaction.

On the other hand, consider a longer-term class that has a definite ending. Members join to achieve a specific goal, such as obtaining continuing education credits or certifications. In such a class, the direction is already chosen, the agenda laid out, and the overall objective defined. The main goal is achieved by accomplishing a number of sub-goals, or tasks, such as presentations, participation, group interaction, and final projects. Teamwork is used to achieve the individual tasks required to complete a project. Tasks may include fundraising, advertising, event planning, researching, and managing social media. Through this teamwork, members bond with and rely on each other to finish the work assigned. Teamwork and creativity are two elements that cement a sense of community.

I joined a community of people that wanted to further their experience with yoga through a yoga-teacher training course. Each person had 200 hours of yoga-teacher training prior to beginning the program. The group met for a full week at the beginning of the program, and also at the end. Between these week-long sessions, we met one long weekend each month for a year. Enrollment ended on the day the training started, and we all began at the same time.

The teacher, not a peer, who facilitated the group, flew into town for each session. He established the overall rules: be on time, participate, sit up during lessons and demonstrations (no lying down), and attend all the sessions.

This community met for a specific purpose for a specific amount of time. Some members knew a few people in the group ahead of time; otherwise, we were all new to each other. We gathered to learn the content of each session, to practice yoga, and to organize and implement our final project – a day-long yoga event in the local community, to be held during our last session of the course.

This community came together for a learning experience. Our interactions with one another included being attentive students, individual participation in lessons, group participation to complete assigned presentations, and group interactions with individual responsibility for completing a piece of the final project.

Informally, we got to know one another through breaks and meals. Formally, we learned about each other as we presented topics and participated in class. Members of the community volunteered to create portions of the day-long yoga event based on their experience, skills, interest, or relevant networking ability.

Our main purpose within the community was to complete a yoga-teacher training certification, but we fulfilled many individual roles to make this happen. As a whole, we needed to learn from one another the skills needed to successfully complete a day-long event, such as registration, sponsor recruitment, logo and t-shirt design, agenda planning, venue selection, timing, marketing, and advertising. We established informal leadership roles within each team, and each member of the team took responsibility for their assigned tasks.

It was a big event to engage the yoga certification community and use each person's skills effectively. We all had to contribute, participate, and learn the functions of our roles. There were definitely times when one person or another wanted to control how a section of the event was handled. We resolved these conflicts through group voting or through the person backing off and letting go of control.

Some of the interactions were not comfortable, leaving members unhappy or in disagreement. Yes, we had differences of opinion and disagreements about who controlled what decisions. There were defining moments when the group made choices and as a community, we proceeded in the decided-upon direction. There was give and take, stepping up and letting go, in order for us to complete all the tasks required to offer the community yoga day. We learned to work together, sometimes by trial and error. We learned cooperation and letting go of control to achieve our goal, which benefitted everyone.

This community had a specific start time and a specific end time in order to meet a specific purpose. Not all of it was sunshine and roses, but at the end, we celebrated a successful day-long yoga event together.

I chose the commonality, the overall goal, and a community arose from this group for a specific purpose – to earn a yoga-teacher certification. There wasn't a formal hierarchy in our teams or in the way they interacted with each other, but the teamwork and creation of the final project determined a structure that formed community. We had to navigate the entry and exit of the sub-committees, meaning there was a time order that each task needed to take place in, and each task was completed by different individuals. For example: When did the venue need to be selected by? At what point in the process did the t-shirt design need to be completed? In order to sign off on the t-shirt design, the sponsor logos had to be available to be printed on the back.

When the program ended, I didn't feel that the community was fulfilling in any long-term way. We each received the certification and the education from the learning experience. The bonds formed and then disbanded, and except for casual contact through social media, each individual returned to their own space. We took what we learned from our experiences and applied what was relevant to our daily lives.

> Women need real moments of solitude
> and self-reflection to balance out how
> much of ourselves we give away.
> – Barbara De Angelis

A community is an organism in and of itself. It has a life force established by the energy, intent, and purpose of its members, regardless of whether the community is finite or ongoing. In transient communities, the entity disbands, and members disburse once the overall purpose has been completed.

Chapter 12:
Community as an Entity

Consider a community as an entity, a whole unit containing interdependent parts. The members of the community are pieces of the whole. The community is a living organism, with an ebb and flow depending on the energy and purpose of the group. Regarding the community as the entity, rather than just yourself as a member, helps define the reciprocity necessary for the community to trust the individual members. I'm talking about what you as an individual give back to the community. The community is like a container that holds the members. If each member sits around and waits for the community to boost them up when the going gets tough, there will be no substance or depth to the community.

How invested are you as a member? Do you just show up? Or do you pay attention to the life of the group by pitching in, arriving on time, respecting confidentiality, and actively participating in discussions and activities? Ask yourself, "What can I bring to the table for other people?" "Is there a function I can take responsibility for within this group?"

In Pam's story, she rallied the right friends from different periods of her life and united them to form a community. An example of reciprocity would be, Pam was able to share her experience of raising two sons through the teenage years with another woman in the group who was having teenage issues of her own at home. At the same time, the group that Pam was instrumental in forming was able to support her as she considered what direction she wanted to take regarding her unhappy marriage.

Regardless of the stated purpose of the community (such as supporting new moms, single women, or caregivers of aging parents), the underlying purpose is meant to bring about change.

> "There is no power for change greater than a community discovering what it cares about."
> — Margaret J. Wheatley

The members interact and engage with each other, prompting change from the current circumstance, whether it is acceptance, reassurance, information, a celebration, or a solution to a problem. These changes bring unity to the community.

> "There is no limit to what we, as women, can accomplish."
> — Michelle Obama

Change may also occur as members join or leave the community. We are all individuals, and the dynamic of a group changes as the members change. Acceptance is a key part of changes in membership.

Community Leadership

A person in a leadership role has a positive effect in the purpose of a community. What type of leadership does your community need? How do you take responsibility for the group by being a leader?

How are leadership and the rules of the community established? Is there a formal or an informal structure? In the single-women group, each host assumed the leadership role for that specific meeting. If the meeting was in your home, you were in charge. In the fitness community, members as a group took responsibility by branching out into activities (jogging, biking, and competing). They decided which exercise modalities to train in and the timing of the training.

Whether the community has an official leader or not, you can lead by accepting responsibility for some part of the community that you recognize needs support. Remember Joan's book club? She was part of the group that organized the book club community from members of a dance class. She created a spreadsheet to organize the direction and rules of the community. She tracked the meetings, the books chosen, and the hosts. Joan took a leadership role within the community. Members stepped up to take responsibility for tasks that needed to be completed. The community trusted the individuals to provide energy, positive attitude, and direction to keep it a healthy, functioning entity.

Leaders often learn from trial and error, but also from experience. You don't have to take a leadership role out of obligation but can choose to participate in something that interests you. Making a difference in your community energizes you and helps you grow and expand your life. Leaders don't come with built-in skills. You may not feel confident or knowledgeable about leadership, but your skills will develop with experience.

Some of the things you can do to lead are help move women in your community forward, improve an existing situation that needs direction, and support the current leader by listening and encouraging. You can also take the lead by modeling cooperation and releasing control in order to achieve benefit for all. Taking action builds your confidence and provides a way for you to give back to your group.

Does leadership play into your needs at this stage in your life? If you aren't comfortable taking extra responsibility, wait until you are in a better place to lead. Do you feel like you can be in charge of an issue, or do you need to play a more passive role for now? If you are overextended in life, you may need to say no to more responsibility. If you want challenge and an active role in the function of the community, acknowledge that goal and take initiative to think like a leader, finding an issue to be responsible for. The members support the community while the community supports the members.

Chapter 13:
Is Joining a Community Worth It?

What personal investment is involved when you join a community? Becoming an active member in a community includes putting yourself out there and keeping your mind open to new opportunities and experiences. The integration period is the time you spend learning about the community, getting to know the members, and putting aside any perceptions you may have until you know what the group is like. You try to understand the rules, and how to fit into the larger community. During this time, you will be "on," putting on your best game face and letting people get to know you, too. You will decide how to contribute and how to get your needs met.

At some point in the process, when you feel comfortable, you will settle in and take advantage of your sense of belonging. You will relax. The following questions can help you determine your degree of comfort. When you interact with the community, are you excited or indifferent? Are you energized or tired? Are you interested or bored? Do you benefit enough from the community to stay a member? You can decide if you are happy and have a fit with the community, or if you want to move on. You have permission to decide that it isn't working for you.

Joining a transient community, like the yoga certification class, requires a time commitment, willingness to cooperate, and teamwork. Your common overall goal means the community has to stay together for the length of the class and has to work together to complete the requirements of the course.

Chapter 14: Your Community Go-forward Plan

Identify what communities or groups you already belong to. Do those communities meet your needs? You may already know what you are looking for and will need to evaluate what feels right to you. Remember Katie's story? She did not recognize that she needed community to support her as she transitioned away from an old relationship. When she realized that community was an answer, she needed help finding social connections and community interaction.

> "One of the most important things you
> can do on this earth is to let people know
> they are not alone."
> — Shannon L. Alder

Some communities naturally come together, such as in a neighborhood, at work, or for a life event. Remember Leslie's neighborhood bunco group supporting her through a divorce? This community was formed because of locality; the women lived in the same neighborhood.

There are many ways to find social connections. Reach out to acquaintances, letting them know what type of community you are looking for or wish to start. Be receptive to their ideas and responses. Are they helpful to your cause? Be accepting of people, because we've all had different experiences in life. Be sociable (yes, even if you are an introvert) to create interaction and connection between you and other people. Give someone a helping hand or be kind to someone who doesn't expect it. Supporting someone else will help you feel stronger and more confident.

Take classes, join a club, or find fun local events. This may sound glib but open up to opportunities that surround you and put you in an environment where you can get to know other women and share experiences with them. Reach out to an old friend. Even if you went through different phases in life, you may be in a place to come back together. Think about Pam and how she re-formed a community by reaching out to old friends. She found that a couple of her old friends were not the type of women she wanted to be around but ended up creating a community of her own with people she wanted to surround herself with.

Put yourself in a situation where you interact with other people, such as church, a fitness center, a class, or a book club. If you do something you care about, you are likely to find women with the same interests.

Research a topic, something you are interested in or curious about. Brittany found what she needed to safely leave her relationship with her boyfriend on a website about narcissism. She didn't know that narcissism described her boyfriend's behavior until she saw the Instagram and began researching the topic.

There are many ways to find connections and community interaction. What other ideas can you think of that relate to your life today?

Learning through your interactions and experiences gives you a sense of belonging and the confidence to help others move forward with more ease. It allows you the benefit of being supported, energetic, connected, and positive. You are not alone. Your efforts will bring you closer to finding the group of like-minded women you want for your community.

Conclusion: Community Makes Your Life Full

We all have similar experiences and emotions as we move through different phases of life. At times, we don't know the next right action to take, and our uncertainty stops us from moving forward. We are familiar with the past and need to navigate the future. Participating in a community provides the means for living life with confidence and ease. You are capable of making a difference in another woman's life. Your life can be positively impacted by opening yourself up to ideas and opportunities other women share. The reciprocity between the give and the take is a life-altering system.

Pam said, "Rather than being open to change, I was waiting for change (in my marriage) to force me to act."

Women Supporting Women:
Redefining Friendship, Tribe, and Community

When have you felt resistance to change? A community can remind you to open yourself up to new people and ideas, and to let go of unhealthy thought patterns. Women in community become a support network to hold you up when fear immobilizes you.

Getting stuck keeps us in place, mostly by keeping us in a holding pattern. We don't want to stay where we are, but we are afraid to experience what the future may bring. We feel like something isn't right, but don't know how to move on. We wait for something external to change when we need to change from within. We are filled with worry and are afraid to make a decision.

Katie said, "I feel stuck! I know the relationship is over, and I can't go back. But I don't know how to move forward." Do you feel stuck? Being in community allows you to express your fear and work through possible choices and decisions that you face. The community helps you identify thoughts and feelings that you need to let go of.

Being overwhelmed can feel like you are not dealing with your emotions, and that they have piled up inside. You may feel like you are not good enough, or that you don't measure up. You may feel like shutting down. You're worried about what you "should" be doing, but you have too many things to do in too little time. Do you feel disconnected from what matters most in life (not laundry)?

Cari said, "Looking back, I was overwhelmed with all the details I had to pay attention to in order to care for my newborn baby. I thought I could just muscle my way through it." Your community can help you make your underlying expectations more realistic. They will remind you to aim for progress, not perfection, and that small steps lead to bigger outcomes.

Needing purpose may be your saving grace. The need for purpose allows you to grow and move away from the past. Keep yourself open to opportunities that make you feel alive or passionate. As an empty nester, Paula felt like she needed more purpose in her life. She thought she had to do something big, important, and meaningful. Average life wasn't enough.

Do you feel like having purpose will add more meaning to your life? Community can remind you that helping others gives you purpose and helps you define how you can make an impact. Community reminds you that gratitude clears the path to purpose. You impact people positively by being authentic and contributing your best. You put yourself in the best scenario possible for moving forward in a positive direction by participating in the right community for you. Community helps you know everything will be okay in the end.

> "Each time a woman stands up for herself,
> without knowing it possibly, without
> claiming it, she stands up for all women."
> — Maya Angelou

Women Supporting Women:
Redefining Friendship, Tribe, and Community

As women, we get stronger by knowing each other and sharing our experiences. Because it's human nature, our thoughts make up stories about our lives. We get a reality check when our support network talks about the truth, even if it feels awkward or uncomfortable. We are directed to stay on the right track.

Forming close connections happens when we share stories, celebrations, and challenges. You will be inspired to find your voice and choose your own way when you have the support of your community. Letting go of uncertainty and anxiety by lifting each other up helps you feel less alone and able to move forward in life with more confidence and ease.

About the Author

Nancy Whitman Klotz is the founder of Balanced Health Yoga Therapy. She has been teaching yoga for ten years and provides private and group class instruction. Currently, she is a Yoga Therapist in training, with Inner Peace Yoga Therapy, and promotes health and well-being for her clients by creating self-care programs that consider the whole person – body, mind, and spirit. Nancy has her Master's in Education, is registered through the yoga alliance ERYT-200 RYT-500 and is a member of the International Association of Yoga Therapists.

Nancy lives in the Midwest, and along with most people around her, really misses the sun during the winter. She enjoys listening to people's stories and feels there is something to learn from everyone. She has two grown children who live in different parts of the country giving her the opportunity to visit fun places.

Learn more about how yoga therapy can work for you by visiting www.BalancedHealthYogaTherapy.com .

Made in the USA
Middletown, DE
25 March 2020